iOS 17 User Guide

A User Manual Based On The Incoming iOS 17 Update
That Best Explores Its Useful Features To Prompt Smooth
Running Of Supported iPhone Devices

Timo Helen

Table of Contents

Section One

Compatibility Note

Support for the iPhone 8, iPhone 8 Plus, and iPhone X has been removed from iOS 17 in favor of the newer iPhone XR and iPhone XS models. These gadgets worked with iOS 16, but they can't be upgraded to iOS 17. In addition to the iPhone 14 and 14 Plus, the iPhone 14 Pro and 14 Pro Max, the iPhone 13 and 13 mini, the iPhone 12 and 12 mini, the iPhone 12 and 12 Pro, the iPhone 11 and 11 Pro, the iPhone XS, the iPhone XS Max, the iPhone XR, and the iPhone SE are all supported (2nd generation or later).

Features available in iOS 17

- iPhone Voice Recording App: Record Your Own

- iOS 17 provides a look of the prior day's weather.

- Activate Spotlight's accessibility tools. iOS 17 font size search for Clock

- In iOS 17, Apple Music has been updated.

- Automatically Enter Email-Based Verification Codes

- Give Your Passwords to Your Close Friends

- Use Siri on iPhone to Issue Several Requests at Once

- Get a Caution About Adult Material

- The iPhone's Clock app has many timers under the Data Usage tab.

- Silence Focus Modes

- iOS 17 has a text magnifier.

- The Safari Incognito Mode

- Auto remove verification numbers

- iPhone's interactive widgets

- iOS 17 introduces AirTag sharing.

- IOS device-based Apple Watch pinging

- Convert images for use as iPhone stickers

- Photo library of People and Their Pets.

iOS 17 Notes

An important new feature in iOS 17 is the ability to give each incoming caller a unique appearance at the caller's discretion.

When the iPhone is put horizontally, the StandBy feature transforms it into a mini-hub for the house, showing the time, date, weather, and even allowing full-screen Live Activities to be shown.

You can perform things like mark items off a to-do list or switch off the lights directly from the widgets on the Home Screen without opening an app. You can now start a SharePlay session simply by holding two iPhones together, and AirDrop has been upgraded to allow for instantaneous contact sharing with the new NameDrop feature. Passengers may now listen to their own music via SharePlay and CarPlay in the vehicle.

Also new this year: an in-app diary, AirPlay in certain hotel rooms, enhanced AirPods Pro 2 with Adaptive Audio, offline Maps, a hands-free version of Siri (through the "Hey, Siri" command), enhanced search, and spotlight. The fall is widely regarded as the release window for iOS 17.

The newest version of Apple's iOS mobile operating system is iOS 17. iOS 17, first announced in June, is now under beta testing and is expected to be released in September alongside new iPhones. All-new journaling app coming later this year; minor updates to existing applications; new capabilities for Phone, FaceTime, and Messages.

Apple redesigned the Phone app with an emphasis on improving phone calls. Understand that the contact information poster recipients view when you call can be tailored to your style. Photo or Memoji uploading, font and color customization, and more are all possible. The Phone app, as well as other apps, may make use of Contact Posters. The Live Voicemail function displays a live transcription of a voicemail on the Lock Screen as the caller is talking. Listening to the conversation might help you decide whether or not to call the person. Spam calls are automatically blocked by carriers and won't go to your Live Voicemail.

With the new feature of AirDrop called NameDrop, you can just bring your iPhone close to another iPhone to swap phone numbers. The Apple Watch is within the sphere of things. By simply touching the screens of two iPhones together, SharePlay is activated, allowing you to share your media library with a friend or family member who also uses an iPhone. Later this year, two nearby phones can begin a huge file transfer using AirDrop, and the transfer can be completed using iCloud.

If you don't answer a FaceTime call, the other person might leave you either an audio or visual message. A variety of Reactions, like hearts, balloons, fireworks, laser beams, and rain, are also available in FaceTime. Gesture activation of effects will extend to third-party apps.

FaceTime on the big screen is now possible with an iPhone, iPad, and Apple TV 4K. With Continuity Camera, an iOS smartphone may be used as the camera during a FaceTime chat, with the footage being displayed on the TV. All of FaceTime's capabilities, including Center Stage framing and Handoff for moving calls between an iOS smartphone and a TV, are fully supported.

The "+" button next to the compose bar in the Messages app now conceals shortcuts to other applications, images, and the camera. You can access the Camera, Photos, Apple Cash, Audio Messages, and your Messages applications with a single tap, as well as the revamped Stickers feature.

You can find every single emoji you could ever want under the Stickers menu of the Messages app. In addition to their regular use, emoji may also be used as a sticker, being applied to other media such as text or photographs. The Remove Subject from Background function, new in iOS 16, allows you to use your own images to make stickers. Using a Live Photo will produce an animated sticker that can be sent using the Messages app. Special effects, such as a hand-drawn appearance, glitter, or a different hue, may be applied to stickers, and they can be used wherever in iOS that an emoji can be.

Messages' search function allows you to narrow your results using various criteria. You may perform a general search and then refine it with more specific terms. The catch-up arrow is helpful if you're having problems keeping up in a group chat or with a person who sends a lot of messages. It takes you back to the point where you last saw unread messages. Swiping on a text bubble will send an instant reply, and voicemails are now automatically transcribed and displayed for instant reading. The Messages app's one-time verification credentials can be erased mechanically.

When a person discloses their location in Messages, the discussion receives an instantaneous update. Together with the Check In safety function, it notifies loved ones that you have arrived at your destination without incident. With Check In on, your contact will be alerted when you arrive at your destination, and if you don't arrive on time or make further progress, they will be able to view your iPhone's location, battery life, and cellular connectivity to determine if you need assistance. A new nudity warning allows you to prevent unsolicited nude photographs from being sent in chats.

In order to better predict what you want to say, Apple updated autocorrect throughout iOS using a new machine learning model. When typing, it can suggest whole phrases to autofill using inline predictions, making it easy to conclude a thought with only a space. Tap-based error correction makes it simpler to fix typos. Dictation has also been improved using a new voice recognition model.

The iPhone's StandBy mode, activated when the phone is placed horizontally on a charger, provides a full-screen display of useful information when you're not using the phone. StandBy mode is most useful with a constantly-on screen, but you can also access it with a tap. It functions similarly to Apple Watch's Nightstand mode, with a variety of clock faces, photographs, calendar and weather options, a glance at Live Activities, and the ability to create your own widgets using Smart Stack.

You can now utilize widgets on the Home Screen to accomplish things like adjust the volume, turn on a light, check off a to-do list, and more. You can do more with Spotlight Search, including adjust settings, without even launching an application.

The Health app's mood monitoring function makes it possible to keep a diary of one's emotional state over time. It will provide tools for keeping track of your emotions and the events that triggered them, allowing you to draw meaningful conclusions. Apple provides clinically-validated depression and anxiety screening tools.

Using the TrueDepth camera and the Screen Distance measurement feature in Screen Time, the Health app can tell you if you're sitting too near to your screen. This is designed for children, but adults may benefit from the function as well; it alerts you if you bring your smartphone any closer than 12 inches to your face.

A new Journal app, planned for iOS 17, will let you to keep track of your daily reflections and actions. The iPhone will utilize its built-in machine learning to recommend things you might want to write about depending on your day's activities, such as where you went, what you did for exercise, who you talked to, what images you took, and so on. All material is encrypted and password protected, however third-party apps can provide journaling prompts.

Safari's private mode is protected by Face ID and prevents websites from collecting data about your Safari activity. Using Profiles, you can keep your professional and private surfing activities distinct, each with its own set of bookmarks, extensions, Tab Groups, favorites, and cookies.

Both Visual Lookup and the Photos app support pausing video so that dogs may be identified. The feature now detects businesses, signs, and movies, and can identify food to suggest related recipes.

The Passwords app has a Family Sharing function that allows users to easily distribute their passwords and passkeys to their loved ones. Using iCloud Keychain, your team can safely exchange and edit passwords across all devices. When several users want access to a password, such for a streaming service, this function comes in handy.

SharePlay in the car allows passengers to contribute songs to what's playing through CarPlay, regardless of whether or not the driver has an Apple Music membership, and Apple Music's Collaborative Playlists make it easy to listen to music with friends. Crossfade lets you seamlessly transition from one music to the next without any awkward silences.

You can now get offline maps of some areas within the Maps app and use them without an internet connection to get directions, an ETA, and information about local businesses and attractions. Apple recently updated its maps to include additional details about trails in parks around the United States, and they also now show the locations of charging stations in real time for electric vehicles.

AirTags may now be shared, allowing many users to simultaneously monitor a single AirTag in the Find My app. The item's location may be viewed by anybody, a sound can be played, and Precision Finding can be used; it also is compatible with Find My network add-ons.

Moreover, later this year, some hotels will enable AirPlay on TVs, allowing you faster access to your entertainment while traveling. AirPlay gets dynamic by learning the device sharing preferences. In order to access your iPhone, all you need is your Apple ID and either a trusted device or a known email address or phone number.

The AirPods have been updated with additional functions. The Adaptive Audio feature of the AirPods Pro 2 combines Active Noise Cancellation with Transparency, allowing you to be more aware of your surroundings while simultaneously reducing the volume of distracting background noise. Music is muted automatically when someone starts talking so you can hear them, and Personalized Volume lets you set the volume to your liking. Sound may be muted and unmuted by pressing and holding the AirPods' stem, and Automatic Switching has been improved to make switching between devices faster and more dependable.

PIN codes and tap to open are supported by Matter-based smart locks, and activity information for up to 30 days is available for door locks, garage doors, contact sensors, and alarm systems via the Home app.

Reminders has a built-in grocery list that organizes your goods into categories, and Notes lets you make internal ties between relevant notes. You can read and annotate PDFs and scans using the Notes app's enhanced PDF capability.

Siri may now be activated with simply the word "Siri," eliminating the requirement to first say "Hey Siri." It is not necessary to restart Siri between successive instructions. It's important to remember that only newer smartphones can activate Siri without the Hey command.

Similar to the Messages app, the Mail app may be set to automatically fill in verification codes. Apple News users may use the Podcasts app to get daily crossword puzzles and Apple News+ Audio Stories.

Highlights of your friends' fitness activities may be viewed in the Fitness app, and with Apple Fitness+

Custom Plans, you can make your own exercise and mindfulness routines. New drawing tools such as a watercolor brush, highlighter, and ruler are available in Freeform.

Live Speech is an accessibility feature that allows written words to be said in person, over the phone, or over FaceTime, and Personal Voice allows users in risk of losing their ability to speak to create a voice that sounds like theirs. To help the visually impaired and the blind, Point and Speak can interpret printed material from real-world items.

iOS 17 Beta Version

Apple does not advocate installing the iOS 17 Beta on your primary iPhone. If you have a second iPhone, use it instead. Because of the nature of beta software, there is always the chance that unexpected difficulties can arise and render the program unusable.

- Create an Offline Copy of Your Device First
- Be sure to back up your iOS device using the following technique before installing the beta software, otherwise you will be stuck on beta version if something goes wrong.
- Connect your iPhone to your Mac using the included cable.

- To allow the item to connect, select Allow from the pop-up window.

- Launch Finder by double-clicking its icon in the Dock.

- Access your iOS gadget's settings by tapping its name in the sidebar.

- If you're connecting your device to your Mac for the first time, you'll want to select Trust in the Finder window.

- Once asked, choose Trust and input your passcode to confirm.

- Select the checkbox beside the option to Back up all of your iPad data to this Mac in the General menu.

- Select "Encrypt local backup" and provide a password to safeguard your data.

- Select Back Up Now if you have already set up encrypted backups or if you do not wish to generate an encrypted backup.

- If you go to the General page, just above the Manage Backups button, you'll see the time and date of the last backup after it's done. Keep in mind that even if you choose to back up your iPhone manually or automatically in the future, this backup will remain intact so that you can always access it using the Restore Backup, on the same Finder screen.

Getting the iOS 17 Beta for Developers

Users who have already joined on Apple's Beta Software Program have the opportunity to download and install the iOS 17 Developer Beta, despite the fact that the program is only intended to be for Public Betas as of this writing. This indicates that the feature is a bug, thus it's probable that Apple will get rid of it. However, if you're already signed up for Public Betas, you may move on to the next section.

1. Get access to developer.apple.com via Safari.

2. Select Account from the menu that appears when you hit the hamburger icon in the upper left corner.

3. Then, input the two-factor authentication code delivered to your devices and click "Sign

in to Apple Developer." Finally, enter your Apple ID and password and submit them using the arrow buttons.

4. Select Account by tapping the menu button twice.

5. Scroll down to Apple Developer Agreement, check the box indicating your acceptance of its terms, then select the "I Agree" button to confirm your acceptance.

6. Verify that you're on iOS version 16.4 or later by accessing Software Update in your iPhone's settings. Restart your iPhone if you have just finished steps 1-5 of creating a developer account. If it isn't, get the most recent update, install it, and let the device restart.

7. Select "Settings" and then "General" and then "Software Update"

8. Use the Beta Versions. Turning off Automatic Updates -> Download iOS Updates and then tapping Back should make the choice visible if it isn't already.

9. From the drop-down menu, choose iOS 17 Developer Beta, and then touch Back.

10. Software Update screen appears.

11. Tap Download and Install when the iOS 17 Developer Beta pops up, then follow the on-screen prompts to finish the installation.

Section Two

iOS 17 Features Detailing

Lock Screen Updates

Apple made significant improvements to the Lock Screen in iOS 16, and with iOS 17, the Lock Screen will be even more helpful than before.

StandBy

The new StandBy Lock Screen option for the iPhone kicks in while the device is charging in a horizontal (landscape) position using a MagSafe, Qi, or Lightning cable. Akin to the Apple Watch's

Nightstand mode, this one transforms your idle iPhone into a mini-computer of sorts.

StandBy mode on the iPhone allows you to view a variety of widgets, including the clock, a calendar, your favorite photographs collected with Memories, alerts, music controls, visual answers from Siri, Live Activities, the weather, and more.

You can navigate through available choices with a swipe to the left or right, and add your own touches with a long tap. You may change the clock's style, alter the photographs that appear, and pick and choose which widgets to show on the widgets StandBy screen. You may use any of your Lock Screen widgets in your StandBy hub, making it completely tailored to your requirements. StandBy is at its most useful when paired with an always-on display, although it can also be activated with a tap on iPhones that don't have this feature.

Interactive Widgets

You may utilize the widgets that appear on the Lock Screen and the Home Screen independently of any apps. For instance, in the Reminders widget, you may mark off completed tasks, and in the Home widget, you can manage your smart home devices. Apple's apps are compatible with these kinds of interactive widgets, and third-party app developers will soon be able to take use of them as well.

Keyboard Changes

In iOS 17, newer machine learning tech is used to enhance autocorrect. Autocorrect learns from your patterns and improves its predictions over time, making them more accurate.

Autocorrect Feature

You may now utilize inline predictions by tapping the space bar to end phrases and even sentences without having to manually input a word.

Autocorrected words are highlighted on the iPhone and iPad once they've been corrected so you can easily see what was modified, and a simple tap will take you back to your original text.

AirDrop Updates

NameDrop is an addition to AirDrop that allows users to instantly share their contact information with anybody else in range of their iPhone or Apple Watch. Send someone your Contact Poster, complete with whatever combination of phone numbers and email addresses you choose.

Proximity Sharing

You may start an AirDrop file transfer by just holding your iPhone near another iPhone, making it easy to send images and other files to a close friend or colleague.

Internet Transfers

You can start an AirDrop transfer using proximity later this year and finish it using iCloud if you have to move away from the other person. Larger files may be exchanged with ease in this manner. It's important to remember that both users must be logged into iCloud for this to function.

SharePlay Initiation

SharePlay is simply activated by holding two iPhones together, therefore, allowing you to share the screen and content with someone sitting next to you.

App Updates

Apple has updated the default applications included with iOS 17 like it does with every major release. Almost every preinstalled iOS software has been updated with additional functionality, including Phone, Messages, Photos, Notes, and Reminders.

Phone App

Phone now has a feature called Contact Posters, which lets you choose what people see when you call them. Choose a photo from your library or use a Memoji as the backdrop, and then tweak the name's font and color to your liking.

Choose a Contact photo in iOS 17 to have it show up in all of your Messages, and now that same feature will apply to your call screen. Your Contact Poster can be kept private or made available to everyone in your phonebook. In order for the other person to see your personal picture, they must have an iPhone. When someone leaves you a message, you may check your Lock Screen in real time to get a transcription of what was said, thanks to Live Voicemail. The next step is up to you: either answer the call if it's urgent or set it to voicemail. Whenever you use Live Voicemail, your voicemail greeting will be updated.

Calls from unidentified numbers are sent to Live Voicemail when Silence Unknown Callers is on, but calls from known spam numbers are instantly rejected.

Call Log

You may now see and access voicemails left by missed and received callers in the Recents call log.

Messages

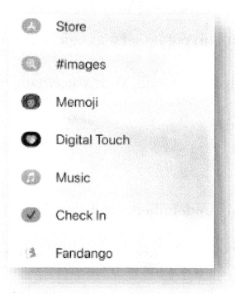

The Messages app has been updated by Apple to have a more streamlined appearance. The "+" button in Messages opens up all available applications and tools, such as the camera and other picture editing choices.

With the new **Check In** safety function, you may inform loved ones of your whereabouts and they will be alerted as soon as you arrive. If you stop moving toward your destination, Messages will inquire as to why and, if you don't respond, will relay useful information like as your battery life, position, and cellular connectivity to the person you're traveling with. You may choose how much information you want to reveal. The difference between the Limited and Full sharing options is that the latter includes the route taken, the latest iPhone unlock location, and the place from which the Apple Watch was removed.

The Stickers interface has been updated, and every emoji may now be found in the same area as other stickers. You can now access emoji, stickers from the

App Store, stickers you've made from images, and Memoji all from the Stickers menu in the modernized Messages app. Messages may now include emoji as easily as stickers.

Sticker Creation

In iOS 16, Apple added a new function called Remove Subject From Background, which may be used to make and save personalized stickers. You may customize your sticker with a variety of frames, fill colors, and even animations using a Live Photo.

Sticker Reactions

Messages may be responded to using emoji and stickers by tapping the sticker and placing it on the conversation bubble.

Stickers in More Contexts - Similar to emoji, stickers may be used in any context where emoji are available, such as in App Store apps, photos, emails, and more.

Catch-Up

When you hit the catch-up arrow in a discussion in Messages with a friend or a group of friends and you are behind, the app will immediately take you to the first message in the conversation that you have missed.

Swipe Reply

Swiping right on a message in a discussion will send a response. Instead of needing to long-press and tap the screen to bring up the reply interface, you can just press here.

Search filter

Because you may now mix search filters, finding what you need is faster than ever before in search. To locate messages relating to your cat, for instance, you might just search "cat," but adding "April" would limit the results to those posted within that month. This function is useful since it allows you to look for messages sent or received by a certain individual.

Location Sharing

You may share your current location with friends or ask them to do the same by selecting the Location option from the "+" button in Messages. If you want to let people know where you currently are or where you plan to go, you may share a pin.

Audio Message Transcriptions

If you get an audio message but are unable to play it straight away, you can view a transcription of it instead.

Auto-Delete Verification Codes

To avoid having to manually erase one-time passcodes from your Messages app once they've been used, you may have them automatically deleted.

Memoji

New Memoji stickers include a halo, a smirk, and a peekaboo.

FaceTime

When someone misses your FaceTime call, you may now leave a message in the form of a video or audio recording, much like a voicemail for a missed phone call. All of the same editing tools, such Portrait mode and Studio Light, are available in your FaceTime video communications.

When you make specific hand motions, FaceTime will react by adding stunning 3D augmented reality effects. Hearts, confetti, fireworks, and other symbols are all represented. The gestures may be used with the front camera on an iPhone 12 or later to access them.

Continuity Camera allows iPhone and iPad users with an Apple TV to use FaceTime on a larger screen. FaceTime calls may either be initiated on an iPhone and transferred to an Apple TV, or initiated from within the Apple TV itself. The iPhone acts as the camera (much like when it is used as a webcam for a Mac), and the Apple TV displays the FaceTime user interface. You'll need an iOS 17 smartphone and an Apple TV 4K running tvOS 17.

Other FaceTime Features

If you miss a call on your iPhone, you may listen to the voicemail or view the video on your Apple Watch.

Journal

Apple is working on a Journal app for the iPhone and iPad that will be available later this year. The Journal app will use data from your iPhone, including photographs, songs, exercises, and more, to generate ideas for entries.

You may highlight pivotal times in your life and add images, music, and audio recordings to your entries.

Both a password and Face ID are required to use the Journal app. All recommendations are made locally, and all data entered is encrypted from beginning to end.

Safari and Passwords

With iOS 17, you may create separate profiles for your professional and personal life by using Safari. Each profile has its own set of bookmarks, extensions, cookies, and favorites, and switching between accounts is as easy as tapping a button.

You may give trusted contacts permission to see your passwords and passkeys in iCloud Keychain by inviting them to view your account. Once a password sharing group has been established, any member may see, modify, and add to the same pool of passwords, ensuring that everyone's credentials are always up to date.

Tracking URLs

To avoid tracking across websites, iOS 17 eliminates tracking parameters from URLs automatically in Safari, Messages, and Mail. In iOS 17, Apple will remove the tracking parameters from a URL while still enabling the link to function normally.

Locked Private Browsing

You can now protect your private browsing sessions with Face ID or Touch ID, making it so that even if someone else gets access to your phone, they will be unable to view the tabs you have open in private browsing. In addition, Apple now completely disables unknown trackers and eliminates tracking applied to URLs during browsing.

Faster Search

Faster response times during searches mean you can see results sooner.

More Relevant Search Results

- Results from a search now include more relevant information presented in a more streamlined fashion.
- Play what Page says

- If you select the Listen to Page option in Safari, the app will read the page aloud.

Maps

In iOS 17, users have the option of downloading Maps for offline use. A section of the map may be downloaded and seen later, even without an internet connection. Information such as store hours and user reviews may be saved, and offline navigation with turn-by-turn directions is possible. The Apple Watch may be used to display downloaded maps.

Charging Stations

Electric car owners may use Maps to see where charging stations are located along their trip in real time. The charging station is user-selectable.

Photos

You can now add your feline and canine friends to the People album thanks to improved facial recognition in the Photos app (Pets and People album).

Section Three

iOS 17 Features Detailing Part 2

Visual Look Up

Now that Visual Look Up supports images of food,

you may use it to find related recipes by tapping the

"Info" button on an image of a meal.

Visual Look Up is available in the Photos app and elsewhere on iOS, such as Safari, for any image.

Remove Subject From Background

You can do a search without leaving the Remove Subject From Background interface when you use it to take an object out of the picture.

Visual Look Up for Videos

To learn more about a certain topic, such as a plant or animal, you can pause the movie at any time by using the info button.

Visual Look Up for Automobile Symbols

Vehicle dashboard icons such as those for hazard alerts, air conditioning, and more may now be recognized by Visual Look Up.

Visual Look Up for Laundry Symbols

Visual Look Up may also be used to decode washing instructions printed on garments.

One-Tap Crop

It is now possible to crop into a specific area of an image while zoomed in on it in the Photos app by tapping the "Crop" button in the top right corner.

Interface Updates

yIn the Photos app's Editing interface, the Cancel and Done buttons have been relocated to the top of the screen, and tool icons have been given text explanations to make their functions more obvious.

Health App

Mood monitoring is one of the new mental health tools available in the Health app. The iPhone's Health app allows you to track your mood throughout the day and in the present.

Determine what contributes to your mood by selecting potential influences, such as job or family, and monitoring your responses over time.

Critical Medication Reminders

Important prescriptions can have a reminder set to alert you 30 minutes after the original reminder if you still haven't taken it.

Screen Distance

Myopia may be caused by holding an iPhone or iPad too near to one's face, which can be detected by the Health app.

The new Screen Distance function employs the TrueDepth camera and is made with kids in mind.

Daylight Exposure for Children

A parent may track their child's sun exposure with the help of the Apple Watch equipped with Family Setup. Health app users may keep tabs on their children's exposure to natural light, which may help reduce the incidence of myopia by 80 to 120 minutes each day.

Mental Health Assessments

If you're worried about your mental health, you can find clinical mental health exams for anxiety and depression in the Health app. Apple will also give links to publications and tools to help you cope with a crisis.

Mail

While there aren't many updates to the Mail app, one handy new feature is the ability to automatically enter one-time verification codes received in Mail into Safari.
One-time verification codes can also be set to expire immediately after usage.

Apple Music

In the second half of the year, the Music app will provide the ability for multiple users to work together to create, edit, and manage a playlist's contents. The function enables users to express their feelings on music with emoji.

SharePlay for CarPlay also enables passengers to enjoy and contribute to the car's soundtrack.

Crossfade

The songs will flow seamlessly into one another without any breaks in the action.

Updated Interface

Albums that are compatible with this new feature will now display animated cover art in full screen, which will also mix in with the music player's controls. The music player's condensed form employs a modern hovering design that includes a depth effect.

Lyric Updates

A bigger, easier-to-read font has been implemented for lyrics that are out of time with the music.

Song Credits

When a song is playing, being searched for, or is in a playlist, you may now hit the three-dot icon to see who performed it. All of the musicians, composers, producers, and engineers who contributed to the final product are included in the credits.

Weather App

The moon module in the Weather app provides information on the moon's phase, the number of days till the next full moon, the times at which the moon will set and rise, and a moon calendar.

Interface Updates

Large "My Location" lettering for your location's weather prediction is displayed on the main Weather page, along with the city name.

Yesterday's Weather

The 10-day prediction in the Weather app has been updated to include conditions from the prior day.

Forecasts

The "daily overview" of the weather conditions includes the possibility of rain for each day over the next 10 days, in addition to yesterday's weather.

Wind Module

The Wind module is a bigger format that provides quick access to data on gust speed, along with daily comparison and a wind scale.

Averages Module

Changes in temperature relative to the daily average are displayed in the new Averages weather module.

Comparisons

Daily UV index, humidity, the "Feels Like," and visibility comparisons are provided.

Units

Wind speed, precipitation, pressure, and distance all have adaptable units.

Reminders

To save you time in the supermarket, the Reminders app can mechanically divide your grocery list into sections. As you fill up your grocery list, goods like fruits, vegetables, milk, and breads are automatically sorted into their respective categories. For instance, the "Produce" section is where you'll find fresh fruits and vegetables, while the "Breads & Cereals" section is where you'll find oatmeal and cereal.

Produce, breads and cereals, frozen foods, snacks and candy, meat, dairy, eggs and cheese, baked goods, household items, personal care and health, and alcoholic beverages are just few of the categories available.

Categories

Grocery lists have categories assigned to them automatically, but you may manually assign categories to other reminder kinds as well.

Column View

Columns may be created to display reminders side by side. Those that want to be organized in a Kanban fashion will find this to be helpful.

Interactive Widgets

Checking off Reminders is now possible directly from the Lock Screen or Home Screen thanks to the use of interactive widgets.

Early Reminders

A reminder alert can be set up to six months in advance.

Notes

You may now create a wiki-like structure by tying different notes together in the Notes app.

PDFs

PDFs and scanned documents may be viewed and annotated in the Notes app. Your iPhone or iPad may now use enhanced autofill to automatically complete forms in PDF files.

Find My

Location Tracking using AirTags and Find Now that my network's accessories may be shared among up to five users, everyone in the family can take advantage of the convenience of sharing AirTags. Precision Finding may be used by anybody with an AirTag to play a sound and locate a misplaced item.

Freeform

The Freeform app for iOS devices has expanded drawing options. There's a ruler, pencil, highlighter, pen of several widths, and two kinds of paintbrushes.

Apple News

Apple News+ members may do crossword puzzles every day in the Apple News app.

Home

New in the Home app is an Activity History that shows recent door, garage door, contact sensor, and security device activity, such as who locked or unlocked it and when.

Lights with a wide color gamut now have an improved user interface, and HomeKit gadgets can be managed with the help of dynamic widgets.

Section Four

iOS 17 Features Detailing Part 3

Wallet App

You can now add an order to your Wallet app directly from an email attachment, and there's a "track with Apple Wallet" button that can be added to websites and applications for tracking your Apple Pay purchases.

Wallet ID Businesses Gray

To prove their age and identity for alcoholic beverages, rental vehicles, and other services later this year, iPhone users will be able to simply pull up their ID through the Wallet app.

Parents may set up weekly, bimonthly, or monthly Apple Cash payments for their kids through the Wallet app.

Apple Cash Recurring Payments

Our separate iOS 17 page for the Wallet app goes into further detail about all of the new features.

Podcasts App

Apple revamped the Now Playing interface so that full-screen covers or episode chapter pictures are displayed. Apple has also altered the playback controls at the bottom of the screen, switching the play speed button and the rewind button places.

Sleep Timer

To make room for the fast forward button, the app's sleep timer button was relocated from the bottom right corner.

Queue Interface

You may now see all episodes in your queue in a list format by pressing the dedicated queue button, which is located at the bottom next to the AirPlay button.

Up Next

The Up Next carousel now has redesigned cards, an options menu icon with three dots, and a new, compact playback indication that displays whether or not a podcast has been begun but not completed. Our Podcasts guide has an in-depth explanation of all the new features in the Podcasts app.

Camera App

iOS 17 includes a refined camera leveling feature. By selecting the new Level option, a horizontal line will be superimposed on the display, allowing you to check that your landscape images are perfectly level.

QR Codes

Since iOS 11, the Camera app has had the ability to scan QR codes; however, with iOS 17, the link button now shows automatically at the bottom of the Camera interface.

Cinematic Mode Video Editing

Cinematic mode video playback and editing capability is available via an API for third-party programs.

App Store App

Once a download has begun, the App Store app will notify you of how much longer it will take to finish.

When you click the "Get" or "Buy" button on an app, the circular download icon will appear and display the remaining time.

AirPlay

AirPlay adapts to your preferences over time, thanks to ever improving in-device intelligence. Therefore, if you frequently use AirPlay from your iPhone to your Apple TV, your iPhone will remember this and prioritize the Apple TV when displaying your AirPlay options. Relevant devices are displayed, and you'll receive proactive connection suggestions based on your previous AirPlay activity.

Airplay hotels

Apple is working with a limited number of hotels to add AirPlay functionality to guest rooms. In the second half of the year, guests at certain hotels will be able to scan a QR code and instantly connect to the in-room television, allowing them to safely exchange films, images, music, and more.

Adaptive Audio

The new AirPods Pro combines Transparency and Active Noise Cancellation into a single mode to intelligently adjust noise cancellation based on your surroundings and interactions with the world around you.

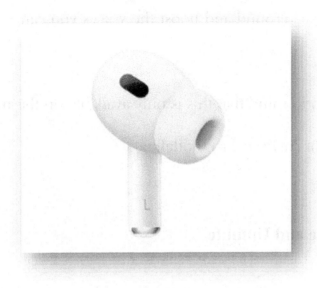

The goal of adaptive audio is to allow you to hear vital alerts and conversations while blocking out unwanted external sounds such as construction noise or airline noise. The iPhone's Personalized Volume feature automatically adjusts the volume of any playing content based on your preferences and the ambient noise level. When a person in the room starts talking, Conversation Awareness will automatically lower the level of the media playing in the background and boost the voices you can really hear.

Keep in mind that this is only available on the most recent AirPods Pro model.

Mute and Unmute

To mute or unmute oneself during a call, just press the stem of your AirPods Pro (or any model of the third-generation AirPods). To control your AirPods Max, tap the Digital Crown.

Automatic Device Switching

Automatic device switching between Apple products saves time and ensures continuity of service. Only the AirPods Pro 2 with an iPhone XR or XS will work. If your iPhone is set to Dark Mode, the AirPods pairing window will also be darkened to match.

Siri and Spotlight

Siri may now be awakened with simply the word "Siri" in iOS 17, eliminating the requirement to say "Hey

Siri." Siri is able to understand and process many queries in rapid succession without requiring a restart.

Ask Siri to let a buddy know you're on your way and then add a reminder to pick up some milk, and she'll do both without you lifting a finger.

App Shortcuts

App Shortcuts will appear in the search results when you conduct a search for an app. Photos search, for instance, will return a Favorites album choice if that's the most often accessed collection.

Search Improvements

Apps that match your preferences in terms of color scheme and icon design will now show up more quickly in search results.

CarPlay

Although Apple has not yet released CarPlay's expected major update, iOS 17 does provide certain improvements.

SharePlay for the Music App

SharePlay is compatible with the Apple Music app in CarPlay, so everyone in the car, including the driver, may add to a playlist while listening to music.

If the driver has an Apple Music membership and starts a SharePlay session via CarPlay, passengers will be able to select songs from their own Apple Music libraries. A QR code created by the primary user allows passengers to view the playlist and add songs to the in-car Apple Music queue simply by scanning the code.

EV Charging Station Improvements

If you drive an EV, you may use the Apple Maps app to find charging stations in your area that use networks compatible with your vehicle in real time. With this upgrade, EV drivers should have an easier time finding local charging stations when traveling.

New CarPlay Experience

The next edition of CarPlay, which will provide even more interaction with automobiles Although Apple did not discuss the upgraded CarPlay experience at

WWDC 2023, the firm did announce in 2022 that the first vehicles will use the new technology by the end of 2023.

Multi Display CarPlay 2

CarPlay will be available on all of a vehicle's screens, including the instrument cluster, thanks to its support for multiple displays. CarPlay will work with the vehicle's instruments, including the speedometer, tachometer, odometer, fuel gauge, and more, allowing Apple to provide a seamless experience across the vehicle.

Next generation CarPlay multi display

In subsequent vehicles, the climate controls will also be accessible through CarPlay, allowing customers to set the temperature and activate other climate settings without ever having to leave the comfort of their seats.

Wallpaper

The new wallpaper settings in iOS 17 may also be used in the CarPlay user interface.

Messages

With CarPlay, reading and responding to messages can be done more quickly and with less distraction thanks to the redesigned Messages app.

Privacy and Security

The new Sensitive Content Warnings feature in iOS 17 allows you to prevent receiving explicit photographs or videos by blurring them before you see them. Messages, AirDrop, Contact Posters, FaceTime, and third-party applications may all make use of the new capability.

Passcode

To prevent being locked out of your device if you change your password and then forget it, iOS now offers you 72 hours to input your previous passcode to reset it.

App Photo Access

If you don't want to give an app access to your whole photo collection, you may choose which individual photographs to share with it.

Calendar Access

The Calendar app now allows third-party apps to add events without seeing any of your private data.

Communication Safety

AirDrop, the system-wide photo picker, FaceTime chats, Contact Posters in the Phone app, and third-party applications are now all covered by the same warnings that appeared in Messages to protect minors from inappropriate content. Additionally, the availability of "Communication Safety" is now global.

Lockdown Mode

The Apple Watch now falls within Lockdown Mode's comprehensive coverage.

Apple ID

An Apple ID-linked email address or phone number, or a nearby device, can be used to login into an iPhone.

Accessibility

Assistive Access makes the iOS user interface easier to navigate, while Personal Voice helps individuals who may lose their speech in the future.

Home Assistive Access

Reduces the bloat of the iOS ecosystem by providing streamlined versions of popular applications like Phone, FaceTime, Photos, and more for the iPhone and iPad.

Live Speech

Live Speech is a feature available on the Mac, iPad, and iPhone that reads the user's typed text aloud during phone calls, FaceTime video chats, and in-person meetings.

Personal Voice

With the use of a random set of text prompts, users of Personal Voice may generate a digital voice that accurately mimics their own. Live Speech allows for the usage of a user's own voice.

Magnifier Point and Speak

You may use the Magnifier app to check the manual for a kitchen equipment.

Voice Control

Users who prefer to type with their voices may now take use of phonetic recommendations for text editing thanks to Voice Control.

Pause Images

In Messages, Safari, and other apps, users who are sensitive to quick animations can stop photos with moving components.

Siri Speed

Siri's voice may be sped up or slowed down by a factor of 0.8x to 2x.

Other New System Features

Several additional minor changes have been made to different iPhone functions that defy categorization.

Faster Haptic Feedback

To make Haptic Touch more resemble 3D Touch, you may increase its speed under the Accessibility settings. If you go to Options > Accessibility > Touch > Haptic Touch, you can enable a substantial speed boost.

Multiple Timers

Multiple timers may now be set and used simultaneously on iOS devices. The most recently set timer will appear on the Dynamic Island and will also be displayed on the Lock Screen.

Ping Apple Watch

If your Apple Watch and iPhone are linked, you may use your phone to send a "ping" to your missing Apple Watch.

Fitness+

Subscribers to Fitness+ may now use the Custom Plans feature to design personalized weekly exercise and mindfulness routines.

Made in the USA
Monee, IL
28 December 2023